HAL•LEONARD
INSTRUMENTAL
PLAY-ALONG

AUDIO
ACCESS
INCLUDED

PLAYBACK+
Speed • Pitch • Balance • Loop

HORN

Christmas Carols

T0081466

TITLE	PAGE
Christ Was Born on Christmas Day	2
Deck the Hall	3
The First Noel	4
Good Christian Men, Rejoice	6
Good King Wenceslas	7
Hark! The Herald Angels Sing	8
I Heard the Bells on Christmas Day	9
It Came Upon the Midnight Clear	10
Joy to the World	12
O Christmas Tree	14
O Come, O Come, Emmanuel	15
O Little Town of Bethlehem	22
Sing We Now of Christmas	16
We Three Kings of Orient Are	18
We Wish You a Merry Christmas	20

To access audio visit:
www.halleonard.com/mylibrary

Enter Code
1769-9582-1665-0214

ISBN: 978-1-4234-1359-2

HAL•LEONARD®
CORPORATION
7777 W. BLUEMOUND RD. P.O. BOX 13819 MILWAUKEE, WI 53213

Visit Hal Leonard Online at
www.halleonard.com

CHRIST WAS BORN ON CHRISTMAS DAY

HORN

Traditional

DECK THE HALL

HORN

Traditional Welsh Carol

4

THE FIRST NOEL

HORN

17th Century English Carol
Music from W. Sandys' *Christmas Carols*

GOOD CHRISTIAN MEN, REJOICE

HORN

14th Century Latin Text
14th Century German Melody

GOOD KING WENCESLAS

Words by JOHN M. NEALE
Music from *Piae Cantiones*

HORN

HARK! THE HERALD ANGELS SING

HORN

Words by CHARLES WESLEY
Music by FELIX MENDELSSOHN-BARTHOLDY

I HEARD THE BELLS ON CHRISTMAS DAY

HORN

Words by HENRY WADSWORTH LONGFELLOW
Music by JOHN BAPTISTE CALKIN

IT CAME UPON THE MIDNIGHT CLEAR

Horn

Words by EDMUND HAMILTON SEARS
Music by RICHARD STORRS WILLIS

Expressively

JOY TO THE WORLD

HORN

Words by ISAAC WATTS
Music by GEORGE FRIDERIC HANDEL

O CHRISTMAS TREE

HORN

Traditional German Carol

O COME, O COME, EMMANUEL

HORN

Plainsong, 13th Century

SING WE NOW OF CHRISTMAS

HORN

Traditional

WE THREE KINGS OF ORIENT ARE

HORN

Words and Music by
JOHN H. HOPKINS, JR.

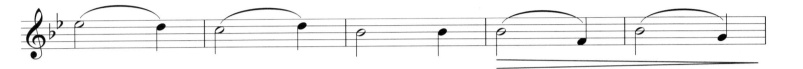

WE WISH YOU A MERRY CHRISTMAS

HORN

Traditional English Folksong

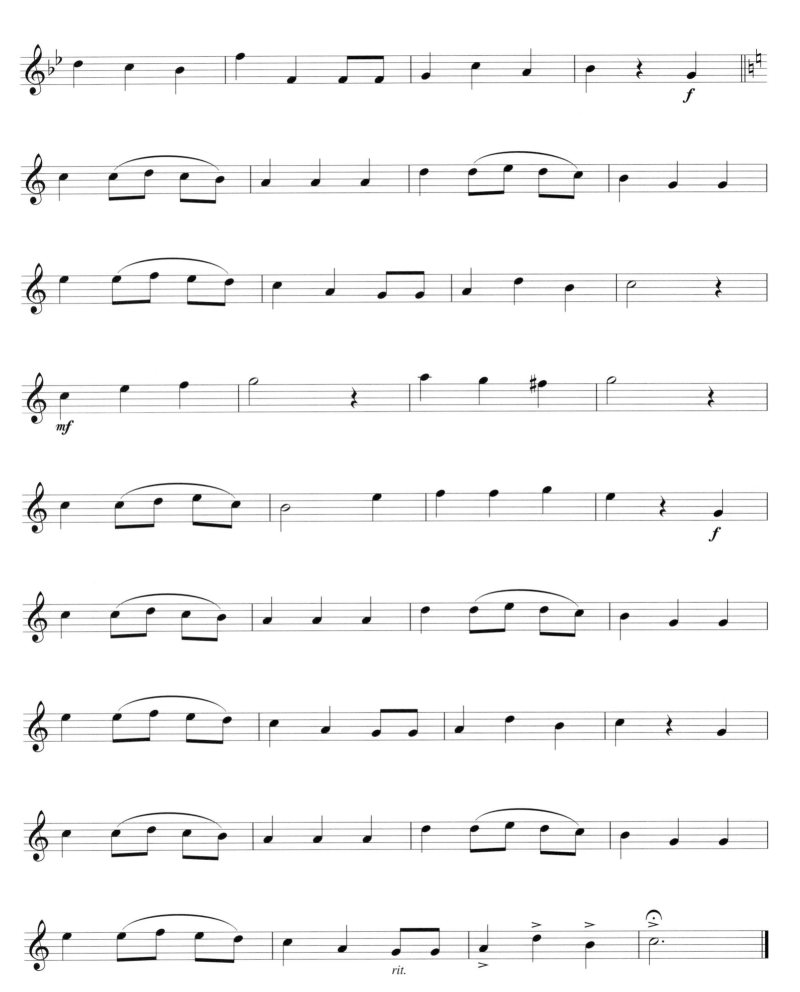

O LITTLE TOWN OF BETHLEHEM

Horn

Words by PHILLIPS BROOKS
Music by LEWIS H. REDNER